ALTERNATIVE LIVES

Alternative Lives

Constance Urdang

University of Pittsburgh Press

Published by the University of Pittsburgh Press, Pittsburgh, Pa. 15260
Copyright © 1990, Constance Urdang
All rights reserved
Baker & Taylor International, London
Manufactured in the United States of America

Library of Congress Cataloging-in-Publication Data

Urdang, Constance.
   Alternative lives / Constance Urdang.
      p.   cm. — (Pitt poetry series)
   ISBN 0-8229-3650-X. — ISBN 0-8229-5439-7 (pbk.)
   I. Title. II. Series.
   PS3571.R3A79   1990
   811'.54—dc20   90-33962
                                             CIP

Some of these poems have appeared, perhaps in slightly different form, in *The First Anthology of Missouri Women Writers, New Letters, The New Republic, Ontario Review, Panoply, Ploughshares, Poetry, Poetry Review, River Styx, Shenandoah, The Southern California Anthology, Tendril,* and *Western Humanities Review.* "Emergency Ward, St. Vincent's" originally appeared in *The New Yorker.*

*The publication of this book is supported by grants
from the National Endowment for the Arts
in Washington, D.C., a Federal agency,
and the Pennsylvania Council on the Arts.*

for Don, in spite of hell and transmigration

Contents

I

Contents

I

Envy of Other Lives

1. Envy of the Artist

To stand in a large, empty room, freezing cold,
Confronting the easel in the eye of a storm of light,
Your only weapon "a kitchen knife
With which to stick layers of paint
On a large, empty canvas," like Courbet
(On the mantel, a bottle and half-empty glass);
Or to be like Monet, who seized the brightness
From a cliff-face, then "plunged his hands
Into a rainstorm, and flung it onto the canvas"—
Like Klee, to live "somewhat closer to the heart
Of creation than usual;" to make a truthful image
Of the world, so that when we go to Holland
We understand everything the landscape says
Because the painters have acted as interpreters,
So that Mexico itself "seems a motif invented
By Diego Rivera;" because
The mystery of the world is in the visible,
And to stand in a large, empty room
In front of a blank canvas, equipped
With nothing but brush and pigment, is to become
An instrument through which the world's remade.

2. Envy of the Cow

Foursquare in the breathtaking landscape,
Dreamy, imperturbable, steadfastly munching,
She does not need to look at the view.
Under her mild brown liquid eye
Earth has set out a lush banquet,
Such succulent flavors and juices
Extracted from acres awash with light,
Rich fields lying tawny and fallow, violet
Distances frosted with cloud
For her to feed on, she is taking it all,

Ruminant mouthful by mouthful,
Sprout, sprig, and blade
Into herself. Now she nibbles away a meadow,
Swallows a hillside, devours
A wood, then a cluster of tile-roofed houses—
Even the highway finds a road
Down her omnivorous gullet, till, having taken
All of it in, the cow becomes part of the scene.

3. Envy of Audacity

Instead of staying in the doll corner
Playing Mother, Father, and Baby, instead
Of cooking and eating, crying and cleaning, to go
Where "the drive to live is stronger than elsewhere,"
To enter the domain of the impossible,
Where foreign tongues take on a libidinal quality
And fraud and deception reveal their dear delights;
To travel roads scarcely marked, tinged
With the faint smell of brimstone, to penetrate
Wild fastnesses where barbaric customs drown
Infant daughters in milk, or let them be trampled
To death, and Christians and Jews
Are impaled or crucified, to dare
To live the fantasies poets only imagine,
Preferring "a dry crust, privations, pain, and danger"
To a life among stiff old houses and historic markers
Where every avenue points to a known destination
And to every adventure's melancholy end.

4. Envy of the Circus

Drawn by the meretricious glitter
Of spangles and sequins, above
The ring's sweaty odors, its glint
Of fools' gold in the dust—

4

To welcome the real brute, danger, that plunges
With the lions into the spotlight, while frolicsome music
Makes light of powerful jaws, to join
The purposeful climb of the aerialist
To the top of the tent, to lean with him
Into the tantalizing rhythms of the trapeze
Is to know with the wire-walker that to be
On the wire is life, and the rest,
The rest, below, is nothing but waiting.

5. Envy of the Past

It's where nothing can harm you; even the painfulness
Of pain, faded like an old snapshot,
Turns emblematic. If yesterday's flowerlike faces
Have power to pierce the heart, it's only
Because we know what they did not foresee
Past the edge of the frame. In the poet's house
Years later, no tremors can still be felt,
And the sadness of old letters under glass
Awakens only an agreeable nostalgia.
Returning to the Loncheria del Ausente
Is no longer possible. Looking backward
Is the only way to experience again
The true feeling of exile.

Alternative Lives

"I could not live like a vegetable in the country."
—Isabel Burton

I could live like a vegetable in the country;
Brushing off crumbs of sleep, the rich loam of dreams,
I'd open one sly eye to the far-off, blue, indifferent sky, swell
In the dark soil, fatten under the moon,
Grow long and pale, or purple as beet, underground;
I could live earthy as a potato, or climb toward heaven
On a trellis, like these beans; why wouldn't
Such a life be sweet?
                              I can picture
Myself in a white apron, shelling peas in a dooryard,
Scattering grain for ducks, gathering eggs
Still warm from the nest. September
Would be the best time, picking apples
From gnarled trees where they'd been ripening
Secretly, in their own time, all summer long.

A Life You Might Say You Might Live

You might call it *a road,*
This track that swerves across the dry field,
And you might call this alley a *street,*
This alley that stumbles downhill between the high walls
And what you might call *doorways,* these black mouths
That open into caves you might call *houses;*
And if you turned at the corner
Into a narrower alley, you might still call it
Going home, and when you got to the place
Where it dwindles to a footpath, and you kept on walking
You would finally come to what you might call *the threshold*
Of a life, of what you might call *your life.*

The Grey Cat

How I envy Mrs. Payne and her husband
Who felt unusual throbbing sensations
A year ago at the Washington Park Zoo
In Portland, Oregon, and knew they were eavesdropping
On the secret code of elephants;
Or Dr. David Gibo, who built a hang-glider
And soared with the monarch butterflies,
Breasting the blue thermals—

For the grey cat is calling, but not to me.
From out of his own wilderness
Only his black-banded banner of a tail
Signals where he is headed under the ghost-pale moon
That, silent and alone,
Continues to sail toward California
Between the yellow flower that opens in the morning
And the *bleu lumière* of afternoon.

The Game of Troy

You want to smash the pattern of everyday,
The dailyness of it, the waking with sticky eyelids,
Feet finding the floor, the toothbrush finding the teeth,
Cold water, then warmer, in the inevitable shower
You don't even remember stepping into, shirt, socks, and so on,
Stairs—and the cat in, or out—
The same thing every day, the same sun
Glinting on fenders and chrome of Fords and Toyotas,
All over the city, people rushing to work with ham sandwiches
Monday to Friday, and weekends at the lake—
Do you think it was different in an age of heroes?
That every day had its dragon? Even on the plain of Troy
Achilles sulked in his tent, and after the fighting was over
Helen would probably have been glad
To go back and be a common housewife.
As for Odysseus, that cunning dawdler,
He invented his own adventures, or Homer did,
Telling tall tales, taking the long way home.

Water Intoxication

Fatherless women who thirst in secret
Have been know to use all the water in the house
Mopping and scrubbing, lunatic laundresses,
Pouring whatever is left down the drain
Or flinging it out the door in a silvery flood
To leave themselves high and dry through another night.

But O in the dewy morning they wake awash
In a watery world, standing all day
Open-mouthed in the shower, or stationed
All day at the drinking fountain, because for them
Water is truly the serum transfusion of life,
Because woman is created out of water.

When a huge wave crashes at their feet
They carefully gather the fragments together
And husband the glittering shards in their cupped hands
And throw them, flashing, back into the ocean,
Mother of waters, and mother of fatherless women.

Robert's Knee

Robert who, more than anyone, abhors
Superstition, and things that can't be explained,
In Manila consulted a psychic surgeon for his knee.
It was in the interest of science.
The house was far out in the suburbs, a long ride
In a rattletrap taxi, with doors wired to close
Like the ones kidnappers use, and upholstery cracked open
To ooze an ambiguous stuffing.

I imagine a house of painted pink stucco.
I imagine a weedy yard with a rusty gate.
I imagine a small, hot room. A single naked bulb
Sways on a cord above the table. I imagine
A woman in a sweaty flowered dress
Welcoming, wearing gold-rimmed glasses. The surgeon enters;
He is a cousin of the taxi driver, small, serious,
In a business suit. He washes his hands at the sink
As the woman positions Robert on the table.
I cannot imagine what will happen next.

It takes a long time. Robert's knee has been examined
By doctors in Denver, St. Louis, and Washington, D.C.
They have attacked it with scalpels and forceps,
They have manipulated it with trained fingers,
They have introduced, through a microscopic incision,
The most advanced instruments, and prescribed
A regimen using pulleys and weights—
Now the surgeon is rubbing his hands over Robert's knee.
It glistens with oil and salve, but Robert can't see it.
Where he lies he can only watch the woman
As she right now touches a match to a single stick
Of incense, and into the corners of the room
Creeps a thin, blue, pungent thread. There is no pain
In the knee, or anywhere, when suddenly
The surgeon raises, with a grunt, a bloody hand
Squeezing something that oozes, something like grit or sand,

11

And displays it to Robert before he flings it, *splat!*
Into a basin. That's it, then.
                              I imagine
Robert sitting up to examine his knee.
It looks the same. There is no incision;
This surgeon does not cut. Since flesh is grass,
It moves aside to let him reach within
And pluck out what offends. He's pleased,
Washing his hands. The woman takes the money.

Next morning Robert wonders if he feels
A brief returning twinge. He can't be sure.

Silvino

Silvino, who promised to be here early
To fix the light switches and install the washtubs,
Instead is scurrying through the town
Searching for switchplates and wire, washers and screws
He knew last week he'd need for the job.
I see him skittering from Vulcan to Esmeralda;
There's a shortage of switchplates. Maybe tomorrow
Or maybe next week, or maybe
In another town, he'll find them. Unpredictably now
These shortages: last month it was toothpaste,
In April, milk. From the shelves in the little shops
Detergents vanish, then cooking oil. Silvino is running
Faster now, he's sweating. At home, too many babies.
When he comes empty handed, his wife blames him.
Not long ago he came courting with hair slicked down,
His arms blossoming with roses and carnations.

Carmen

Carmen asks if it is cold, now, in my country.
She wants to know how far it is to where I live.
She wonders if the people there have work,
If they have money, if they have toothache.
Is it a hard journey?
Would it be possible for her to go there?

There are no words for what I have to tell her:
There is no road for her to where I live.
The bridges are all washed out, the highways flooded;
Even in blistering heat my country is cold.
The people have barred their doors against her children,
And there is no room for her at their tables.

Mrs. Mandrell and the Water Table

On the day the well ran dry
Mrs. Mandrell bathed in soda water
Icy and scentless as the mountain spring
Where it erupted and was bottled
Then trucked to her where she lay.

Did its barrage of bubbles
Prickle against her skin?
Did she fizz all over like imported champagne?
Did her body become strange to her,
Suspended in Perrier water?

Luminous in crystal, her body is immortal
In a thousand museums and galleries,
But Mrs. Mandrell is not a renewable resource.
Being writ on water, ambiguous element
From which life springs, when all the wells run dry,
With what shall she be watered?

Frida and I

Following a freak accident that impaled her on a steel rod and doomed
her to a life of pain, Frida Kahlo (1907–1954) became a painter.

Walking into my life one morning on Riverside Drive
With no idea of what to expect, how could I have foreseen
Maguey with tall stalks like giant asparagus
Exploded at the tip into bonsai shapes
Like the windswept pines of northern California,
Or these seminal pigments, crude primary yellows,
Magenta of bougainvillaea, scarlet and vermilion,
Acidic olive greens, puke greens, pinks, purples,
Green-bronze, nut brown, cinnamon, that exhale
An acrid smoke into the thin blue air?
                                          In a black doorway
A girl teeters on spike heels, waiting for her life.
She can't imagine how it will arrange itself
Or what it will offer her. Frida never saw
The accident that created her, changing her in an instant
That never ended, into art. Below the scaffold
Where Rivera painted, she came with her basket, *folklorico,*
Or lay immured in plaster, her screams translated
Into paint, *Frida* after *Frida,* a procession
Whose heroine was death, "little aunt of the little girls."

Death is no stranger in Mexico,
Whether in the blue house on Londres Street
Or in the square near the university
Or in the room never mentioned, behind the police station.
Even in New York it followed her
Through the open window of Hampshire House
Three giant steps down to the sidewalk, as she painted it.

In Paris, she had appetite for the food
But none for the French, and returned inevitably
To the land of the prickly pear, spiny fruit of Mexico
In a parade of self-portraits. They bleed not only
For Frida, but for all she knew, sisters and brothers
Pierced by the thorns of history,
Struggling in violent times to make a life.
Every poem is a self-portrait.

A Little Elegy

for Miriam

1.

When she left, it was without the customary preparations.
The house was in a curious disorder;
No trunks were packed, the dishes left from breakfast
Still stood on the table, and in the upstairs bedrooms
Beds yawned in dismay. How unlike her it was
To embark on such a long journey without making all the
                                    arrangements,
Storing away the things that would not be needed
In closets and attics, everything in its place.
She is gone taking nothing, without saying goodbye,
Leaving in the house an emptiness
That will not be filled.

2.

I thought I would make a wreath
Of the dark green leaves of the homely little plants
She tended with such faithfulness,
Interwoven with mysterious messages, overgrown with the moss
Of old German fairy tales,
Hung with the volatile syllables
Of the French language, strung
With lighthearted ribbons of the baroque,
Music of hautboy, viola da gamba, continuo.
But, clumsy-fingered, I only have these words
To hang on the empty air.

3.

She was one with the mothers
Whose children have disappeared. She was one with those
Who come carrying in a single bundle
All they have in the world, across invisible frontiers.
She stood alone, like a tree
Which is always alone, even when it is surrounded
By other trees. She wept alone in her room.

18

4.

Let rain be her requiem.
The steady unemphatic drizzle
That drenched the mourners on the pale hillside
Where they lowered her ashes into the sodden earth;
The monotone of the dull rains of December;
Crescendo of an equinoctial storm;
Soft summer showers, that sigh the night away
In the garden abandoned beyond weeping windows.

Magritte and the American Wife

In the artist's studio she was amazed
To find furniture such as you might see
In any bourgeois apartment.
A patterned carpet, and curtains at the windows;
The artist himself, "tightly buttoned
Into a dark business suit,"
Thick, rather than fat, short, middle-aged,
Fit disappointingly into his surroundings.
Only the spotless easel betrayed him.

When she asked if he didn't
Get paint on the carpet, he told her he applied
The paint to the canvas, having thought out
In advance, where he would put it.
It was only then she noticed, growing
On a prim Victorian chair,
A lion's tail, and, concealed
In the domestic architecture,
The naked glowing torso of a woman.

Robert's Friends

A host of invisible presences, they are everywhere,
Robert's friends, swarming like gnats
Or shrinking into corners
Like dust mice that have escaped the broom;
When you least expect it you might stumble over one
On the stair, or surprise them in your room.
The air is full of their voices, a muttering descant
Not unlike the speech of elephants, "resembling
The vibrations from the lowest note
On a big pipe-organ, or the slight shock wave
From far-off thunder," something felt
Rather than heard. When Robert leaves,
A palpable absence swells in the house,
As if a glittering procession had just passed there,
A parade with floats and drum majorettes and bands,
Leaving only the echo of trumpets and marching feet
And a barely perceptible troubling of the air.

For the Girl They Tease with the Name "Lizard"

My love, my loving, my lizard-girl,
Beautiful and strange as a lizard,
Fragile, scale perfect in detail,
Fire-breathing, quicksilver-quick
As a lizard,
Which is a dragon in miniature,
Which swiftly climbs the wall on soundless feet,
Which stretches itself in the sun,
Which vanishes into the wall in search of darkness,
Consider how many monkish imaginations,
My lively, my lovely, my jewel-eyed,
Cloisonné-mailed, cloth of gold,
Field of a thousand flowers,
Lizard, you have illuminated.

Son

It is fitting for the son
To go out searching,
To look for his life
Along treeless interstates,
In dull industrial cities,
In towns sucked dry by the wind
And circled by farms
Called Stony, Bleak, Hungry, Desolation;
He thinks of a hillside pasture
Under the rain.
He thinks of pitching a tent
Near an inland stream.
He thinks of piano bars
And little cafés
Under striped awnings,
And sleek acquiescent girls.
He thinks of having everything,
And of the freedom of having nothing.
He will be a millionaire
At twenty-five.
He will put on a tie
And be punctual.
He will be a man.
He will walk up the street hatless
Thinking about his life.
He will wonder
If this is what he meant.
Now he holds the clues
In his hand, a cryptogram
He can't decipher.

My Father's Death

He knew it was waiting for him   somewhere
His own death   that he had sailed to meet
Years ago in Flanders   he never spoke
Of that broken appointment
But throughout the years that followed
He looked for it   among the frail shells
On the beaches of Maine and Connecticut
Or in the pages he loved   of books heady with mildew
Sometimes he forgot it
Till it nipped at his leg   almost playfully
Where the shrapnel still festered
When he was a boy, weak-eyed   in long black stockings
He heard its voice in the sound of milk carts
Grumbling over the cobbles   in his mother's breathy sighs
In the clatter of the el trundling over the points   later
He thought he had outfaced it at the Polyclinic
But he still had a thousand miles to go
To find it   reaching out to take my hand
His own grew cold   and stiffened in the clasp
Of the inevitable last embrace

On Rereading the Poets

Thinking about the mad poets,
The drunken, the drugged, the dead poets,
The forgotten ones, those half-remembered
For badly remembered lines, misunderstood,
Admired for the wrong reasons, and too late,
I am amazed at the persistence of poetry.

Like the secret writing of children
That becomes visible on paper held over a flame,
Obstinately, the old lines come to life
Letter by letter, stuttering across the page,
Confounding criticism, fanned into breath
Over and over, making themselves new again.

This Poem

If you are cold, this poem will not warm you.
If you are hungry, you will not be fed
By this poem; if you are sick
It will not cure you. If you are alone
The poem won't take your hand.

This poem lives in warm houses;
It has never known hunger. All it can do
Is, from a pocket of loose change
Select a coin to drop into your palm,
The cold coin of compassion in this poem.

The Apparition

When the head of Jesus appeared on the bathroom door
Nobody wanted to believe it, but there it was,
Gradually developing like a bad negative,
Those flowing locks, those deep, compassionate eyes
Darkening on the plain wood of the door
Where nothing but the grain of the cheap pine
Had been visible before.

This happened in an ordinary house
Built about eighty years ago, by a man
Who built several others in the neighborhood.
All of them are still lived in, but of course
There have been changes—though in none
Had any kind of apparition
Ever been seen before.

Since no one reported it, nobody came
To kiss it or chip holy splinters off the door,
Or wait for it to weep miraculous tears
And cure cancer or reverse a fatal course;
In any case, it would have been too late
To save my friend, who died suddenly last year
Not having been ill before.

Four Ways to Spend an Evening

1. Sending an Invitation to the Muse

There's no one here; see, we could be alone
In an ambiance of—what did he call it?
Luxe, calme, et volupté—or, if that's too French,
Let's just say I'll provide the place and time.

The place: a high white room all glass and sky
A cube of brightness glowing amid the stars,
Aladdin's cave of marvels in the air,
All richnesses and wonders. You and I

Alone would share the secrets of a time
Outside of time, where no clocks bleat the hour
Or signal starts and stops, or ever change
One season for another less condign.

Apollo, Muse, whatever name you like,
Come soon, outrun the slow horses of the night.

2. Observing the Motion of the Planets

You and I alone have considered the heavenly bodies,
Naming the constellations *scorpion, lion, bull,*
And charting their movements; these clear nights
No special equipment is needed
To pursue their imaginary paths, or study the life
Of a star, mysterious and mathematical
In the far wastes of space. Navigating
As the night birds do on their long journeys, tonight
Let us follow the apparition of Venus
And the slow declination of Mars
Which will reach opposition in September
When it is low in the east at dusk, and visible
All the long night long, to wakeful lovers.

3. Diverting the Company with Games and Music

Generally speaking, it is easier to lose
Than to win, or so it says
In the book of hard-to-follow directions. However,
The only way to play
Is to plan on winning. White sits here,
Black there. The first move
Is determined by chance
(If there is any dispute
Over who will be Black and who White,
That too will be decided
By a throw of the dice).
Following that, it is necessary only
Always to keep the odds in mind.

Luck plays a minor part
According to the book,
Like the troubling little theme
That now and then intrudes on the serene
Progress of the concerto — Mozart's Fifth
For orchestra and piano. One bad move
Is all you need, to lose.

4. Listening to the Voices in the Rain

If a woman walks past, black-shawled,
No figure of antiquity, but worn,
Her face pitted with grief,
Hers is the voice in the rain, whispering
In a language for which we have no words.

What begins as a murmur, barely distinguished
From the gossip of the wind in the leaves
That hints at much more than it ever tells,
Becomes a veritable oration, then an oratorio
For hundreds of voices, solo, duet, and chorus.

Now crescendo, now forte, staccato, diminuendo,
As if numberless black-shawled women have given tongue
In the rain that thrums all night among the leaves
To counterpoint the plainsong of their lives
That comes to us in echoes, if we listen.

The Other One

It's possible the other one's left-handed;
I've often suspected it. How else explain
A certain characteristic clumsiness,
An awkwardness that seems willful, as if determined
Not to perform, with a series of smooth gestures,
In the expected role, but instead to be gauche,
Louche as a wildling, unkempt, undomestic?

The other one's an orphan, no father or mother;
The other one's savage, not stopping to cook the meat,
But tearing it from the bones,
Ready to bed on straw, or leaves, or stones,
With any passing stranger, or with no one.

Unwelcome as a gypsy in a green wagon
Set down on the rubbishy rim of the world;
Not caring to be understood, or misunderstood,
Unblushing, unsexed, capricious as the weather;
Yes, probably left-handed.

Keats

Tomorrow I'll sit out with the poets
On our hard chairs
And let them sing their songs of despair and consolation
Into my left ear

I'll listen to them
Recite sad histories, their brave syllables
Echoing in my right ear

Sitting between
The philosophy of the porch and the
Sophistry of the garden, I'll understand
It isn't Keats I love, but the incorruptible
Purity of his words

I can let that clear flood wash over me
Like a fast-flowing stream over stones
Or lose myself in the luminous eye
Of a single stone, diving into its bottomless depths

II

Traveling Without a Camera

Imagine traveling without a camera.
How difficult it is, trying to remember
Precisely, the pattern stamped by the toothy ridges
At Real de Catorce, against an apricot sky,
Or the look of the mountainside as night overtakes it,
Reclaims it, and salts it with stars—
Which after all are not stars, but the lamps of home
To strangers you never saw and will never meet;
Or to conjure up, to what they call the mind's eye,
The exact configuration of this wall,
Weathered and crumbling, into which a lizard,
Mysteriously, vanishes.
                         Isn't this the way
You traveled through childhood, retaining only
Certain images that at first seem clear
And real as this morning, until you peer
More closely, and they disappear? Deceitful memory!
Fades and dissolves in all around I see,
As if an inept cameraman were to film
Ineptly, for a thousand thousand days,
And leave a darkroom filled with damaged prints.

Ways of Returning

Returning through the back streets, through alleys so narrow
The walls of the houses part like grass,
Leaning backward, their patience demonstrated
By scarred plaster, worm-eaten sills, and
Thrust through a chalk-blue door,
A clenched brass fist, everything the same
As it was, the sun, boys shooting marbles the same,
The same flies buzzing minarets of garbage, the same fists;
Or skating across the enormous mirrored spaces
Of an airport, in St. Louis or anywhere,
Passing the snack bars, the Budget Rent-a-Car, electronic games,
Seeing the men and women queued up to telephone
To say to someone, to anyone
At the end of the line, Hello, it's me,
I'm back; or, after driving all day long
To come into town at nightfall, the avenues
Festooned with lights, every block so familiar
You catch a glimpse of yourself coming down the street,
Yourself, in a coat you wore then, carrying something
You carried then, or maybe are carrying still.

Mornings in Mexico

The sun behind a cloud, the moon behind a tree;
On the speckled pavement
A lizard scurries without sound
And waits, with inexhaustible patience.

Here is a spray of butterflies,
A trembling mosaic of wings:
Take it, take it. Nearby
Invisible as the air, a bird is singing.

This is no time for brooding over old wrongs;
Sighs, sighs—what a wearisome litany.
See where the plain is crisscrossed with goat tracks
All the way to the twilight-colored mountains.

The Blue Door

Think of the sea as a lover,
A single salt kiss dragging you
Through monotonous green depths,
Or the sky, that the child paints
As a strip of blue at the top of the paper
When all around you in the blooming
Buzzing confusion a painting
Is waiting, or a poem:
"Some pomegranates broken open on a plate,"
One battered shoe, a tangle
Of wire coat hangers dangling from a nail,
And suddenly something wants you
To walk down this street
To the house with the blue door
And stand patiently waiting for it to open,
Confident that it will open.

The Gate

Here is the gate,
Maybe not as you imagined it;
Not an ornate affair of painted iron
Offering a tantalizing view
Between tall, welcoming pillars.
No, this gate stands like a barrier across the road,
Bland, imperturbable, indifferent,
It refuses a glimpse of what lies beyond.
It does not want to let you in.
Maybe it conceals a wilderness
Of weeds and rubble. Maybe
A broken fountain, drooling a thin thread
Of water from its cracked lip.
Maybe a sudden surge of hummingbirds,
A flight of butterflies rising on golden wings.
The gate protects its secrets.
There will always be those
Who prefer a walled garden
To a public park full of peonies and roses.

The River

Even here we have driven the river underground;
Not because we didn't admire its icy clarity,
Like glass, that scarcely bent the light of the sun;
Or because we didn't want to refresh ourselves
At its bubbling fountain,
Or bathe in it, where it purled over the stones
Singing to itself its endless song;
Not because it didn't water the plain
And carry off our refuse, washing away
The traces of our picnic on the planet;
I have seen it race like a black torrent
Down the steep channel of the street.
I have heard it roaring under the rain,
And searched for it through the dry days, hoping
For a token to show it would return.
But now it is buried under paving stones,
Deep in the rocks from which it sprang.
In the darkness it hisses and mutters, feeling its way
Like a blind man on an unfamiliar street
Tapping his path between strangers.

Instead

When the pattern changes, instead of a porcelain blue sky,
A sky like a thick woollen blanket. Instead
Of shadows with crisp black edges,
A flimsy grey veil. For "brown, dry, hard,"
Read "green." For "thirsty," read, "flowers."
When the sun emerges it is as a shy young girl
Peering from behind a curtain.
The peach tree offers a basket of fruit.
Splinters of glass in the rubbish heap
Glisten like dew, like diamonds, like
The first morning of the world.

This Life

Here we live mostly outdoors, even in the rainy season;
What is more delicious than the taste of a single raindrop
                                        on the tongue,
Or lovelier than raindrops inscribing their perfect circles
                                        in the fountain,
Or more musical than the little fugitive airs
Rain plays on the flagstones or the leaves?

Here there are houses like caves. A woman like me
Lives in a house dug out of the hillside. All day
She stoops over a smoky fire, or bends to her washing;
At night she reads poetry (spelling out each word
With a laborious finger)—I said she is like me.

Here nothing is welcoming or soft. Along the road
Other women sell creatures in paper boxes, or spiny fruit
Gathered from trees full of thorns, and the sunlight is harsh
Like the land, and the people go with masked faces
To the market, and back to their dark small houses.

What is there here to love? In winter the wells run dry
And the square overflows with tourists. Night after night
The town lights a conflagration against the darkness,
Darkness that surrounds us and would like to swallow us
As if we did not live here, as if we had never lived here.

Green Study in a Dry Climate

I am ashamed at having forgotten the name
Of this plant with its showy crimson blossoms
And shiny leaves, its stiff brown arms extended
So trustingly; I chose her myself
From among all the others, standing like orphans,
Their poor feet wedged into kerosene tins,
Beseeching faces turned toward the sun;
I took her home and fed her,
Put her on a pedestal—and she is still blooming,
But I don't remember her name.

                   ✿

And this cactus: wouldn't he protect me from my enemies?
With his clublike arms, his stubby elbows and knees,
His blunt green fists upraised, each one a bludgeon,
Wouldn't he ward off attackers? Tall as two men,
His thorny bulk bestrides the flagstones, a thousand spikes
Poised to impale. In the embrace
Of those spiny tentacles, this sentinel
Could clasp a dozen malefactors, bad men worse
Than the ones in the sad jail
Who twice a day are marched out to look at the sky
Before going back into puke-smelling cubicles
For another night of darkness and bad dreams.

                   ✿

It's clear one of the old gods
Has come to perch in the mesquite,
Having assumed the shape of a boat-tailed grackle.
He is admonishing me in a language

I don't understand, his peremptory voice
All rattles and squeals.
As the garden fills with the scent of burning
From some ancient sacrifice
I hope it is pleasing to him, his silhouette
Against the sky is so black, sharp, and imperious.

❀

I have agreed to love this poinsettia, even
When she is not in bloom, through the long months
When she offers me only a tangle
Of madder-tinted leaves. I won't imprison her
In a dark cellar, or hide her in a closet
Like some miserable Kaspar Hauser, to force her
To flower; even when she is not beautiful
I will keep her beside me,
Her downward-pointing leaves with their five sad points,
Her lugubrious brown stalks, until one day
Once more she presents me with her single outrageous blossom.

❀

What I need is a garden advisor,
An old man wise in vegetable ways
Who calls the plants by name, and talks with them; I need
Someone who knows when the moon
Is ripe for planting, I need a guide
Through this jungle I've stumbled into
By luck and love, this overgrown Eden, this intemperate land.

44

Salt Dreams

Here, the long growing season means slow starts.
Fresh water spills over the dam, and a hard rain drums,
Pounding, on the roof, and springs out of the waterspouts
Till the clouds are wrung dry in the strong wrists of the air.
If air were my element, I'd float in it
Like the egrets, who lift themselves clear of the heavy earth
On enormous wings spread like sails to catch the wind
That blows a salty breath from the distant ocean.

Far from salt water, I call up the gray-blue Atlantic,
Its attack and retreat on the shore, its crashing
Even when no one is there to see it or hear it,
On the black seaweedy rocks, like a froth of marble,
Its slowly gathering swells, its gathering power
Under a surface deceptive and smooth as a mirror,
Its rollers and breakers, its glittering little crests,
White horses leaping under the whip of sudden squalls.

Salt seasons the little dooryard gardens back there,
Crowded with old-fashioned blossoms of hollyhock,
Marigold, zinnia, cosmos, petunia, lily,
Commoners all, jostling one another
To their clamshell borders; it was salt on the wind
That called the little mermaid back to the sea
That never waits or is still for anyone,
And offers neither caresses nor consolation.

The Salt Museum

In the Salt Museum
Every sculpture, every carved artifact
From the massive heads and torsos
Of giants and giantesses
To antique pieces of furniture
And the most delicate
Filigrees, even fabrics
As fine as cobwebs
Is confected of salt

Here come the visitors, weeping
Wives without husbands, children
Crying for their mothers, lovers
Left lonely, to water with their tears
The displays in the Salt Museum

Each glistening teardrop, evaporated
In the museum's dry air
Deposits an infinitesimal film
On the masterpieces
In the galleries of salt

Winter Gardens (1)

Here is a little garden under glass—
Its mosses like tiny trees, its delicate ferns,
Its pebbles carpeted in lichen velvet,
Even the red-and-black Japanese bridge
That curved from nowhere to nowhere
And the flat, gray-speckled rock by the mirror pond
And the spotted salamander who lived there—
We made it years ago, without a thought
For what might lie over the curve of the bridge
In the mazy future, but took the salamander
Back to the wood to live under a root
In the odor of damp twigs and leaf mold.

Winter Gardens (2)

Everyone knows there are countries
Where winter never comes
Where language has no word for winter

In that eternal April blossoms spring up
Urgently out of the passive soil
To embroider the air with exotic aromas

On a sunny wall
A lizard waits as patient as a stone
No harsh winds steal leaves from those trees

In those countries the seasons change
Only from oleander to hibiscus
From mango to pomegranate

While here Persephone retreats
To the darkness underground
And in winter gardens earth dreams of April

Winter Gardens (3)

When this garden was made to flower under glass
Nobody thought to set out a breakfast buffet
Where now ladies in flowery scarves
Anticipate the season
Picking and choosing among delicacies

If outside the ground is frozen hard
And beggarly December taps on the cold glass
Under the lights heat rises
From the little flames below chafing dishes
For ladies blooming in the unseasonable garden.

Pete and the Drunkards

If he had boarded the bus
With its cracked seats of imitation leather,
Keeping in his hand the flimsy ticket
For which he had paid eighty-five cents American—
That ticket with its meaningless mysterious numbers—
Couldn't Pete have stepped off into this dusty square
With its six withered trees and eight benches?
Couldn't he have walked up this alley
And rented a room in one of these small houses
Where he could unpack his satchel on the thin mattress
And leave his book on the wooden table?
Then under Mexican trees rattling in the wind,
Distraite, waving their wild green arms,
He would have found his way to a lighted doorway
And reeled with the drunkards down passages of stars,
Adrift in the Milky Way, three thousand miles from home.

At Frank 'n' Helen's

It's Nostalgia Week at Frank 'n' Helen's:
The two cops at the table near the door
Ordering pepperoni pizza have hung up
Their two blue coats, and on their brawny thighs
Their blunt black holsters dream. Under tinsel stars
Left over from Christmas, a party of seven,
Every one a senior citizen,
Is making itself at home. Over baskets
Of steaming fried chicken or shrimp
Carried by waitresses gently perspiring,
Sweethearts and strangers catch one another's eye.

Here, in the odor of down-home hospitality
Dispensed for a price (but reasonable),
America rediscovers itself, all the homely virtues
Displayed in the mirrors behind the booths
Where time has been arrested, and everything
Remains what we recall, as Frank—or Helen—
Dreamed it. Here we are all fed, we can all
Love one another. Let the scarlet hearts
Festoon the ceiling, let the walls leaf out
With mammoth cardboard shamrocks, greener far
Than anything in nature, under the dreaming stars.

The Old Ladies of Amsterdam

Indomitable, in black stockings, the old ladies of Amsterdam
Are pedaling their bicycles on the way to market.
Returning, with a chicken and some radishes,
How neatly they thread through the traffic,
Skillfully weaving in and out,
Dark figures in a sunlit tapestry.

Here are the canals of Amsterdam:
Green, sluggish, and redolent of gasoline.
It is raining on the canals. In January
They freeze. From across the Atlantic I see
The old ladies of Amsterdam balancing on silver skates,
Their black skirts whipping around their knees.

I think I am with them. Haven't I felt
A punishing wind bruise the afternoon
On a deserted block that had not been imagined
When Amsterdam was old? Behind an apartment window
An old lady is pouring pale tea from a Delft pot
In the honey-colored light of Vermeer.

Paris

Forty years later she is still the girl
Who lusted after Paris from the Left Bank,
And called from Montmartre,
Where is Paris?
The boulevards did not convince her;
Those French men and women
Marched like a scene from a film,
Black-and-white, moving unevenly,
A little grainy.
In no bistro, in no metro station
Was the true nature of Paris revealed to her.
It was not in the red geraniums
On the balcony of an apartment
Whose dark windows opened on a mysterious life.
It was not in the medieval alleys
Stinking of ancient urine,
Or in the grand hotels;
Not in the museums,
Not in the soft French sky.
Would it have been the same
To have stayed home in Manhattan, dreaming
Of entering a painting by Utrillo
Or a photograph by Cartier-Bresson?

Emergency Ward, St. Vincent's

I think they have brought me by mistake
To the Charity Bird's Hospital in Old Delhi
To be cared for like a wounded pigeon or chicken
Or to the infirmary in Morocco
Where they treat injured storks

I am lying here looking up at the yellow ceiling
At the sweating walls, and down at the tiled floor
In the cubicle next to mine something is moaning
A tough old bird is wheeled in on a gurney
And hidden behind a curtain

Now looking up I see a border of faces
Intent on a part of me beyond my view
They are nodding and muttering to one another
Poets have died before in this drafty ward
Among the diseased and the damaged

Outside in the street a purple dusk is falling
Someone is waiting in the cold corridor
For news of the accident (there is no news)
I could cry out, but instead I lie here suspended
Waiting for pain, for the reappearance of pain

Visiting the Ruins

There are ruins everywhere, both
The old romantic kind, thrusting up
Out of a mist-shrouded German lake
Or those heaps of glass and rubble in Beirut,
Garbage rotting on the avenues of Manhattan,
That don't stand for anything;

A hundred years from now they will all be one
With the buried cities of Troy, the way
Nobody now remembers the war in Spain,
And in the *Book of Compassion and Despair*
Nothing remains but scenes of sorrow and joy
Commemorated like historic sites.

So something's to be said for staying home
And reading Apollinaire in St. Louis
For translating Baudelaire in Iowa City
And looking for Rabelais in secondhand bookshops
Below Fourteenth Street
Without putting a *moi* in every landscape.

Returning to the Port of Authority:
A Picaresque

Some New Yorkers refer to the Port Authority Building, where all buses enter and leave New York, as the "Port of Authority."

1.

Where are they going, the crowds that pass in the street?
I had not thought life had undone so many,
So many men and women, seeking the Port of Authority,
Safe anchorage, harbor, asylum.
                                    Late at night
Theirs are the voices on the radio, asking the hard questions;
Or they don't ask. The homeless, the hunted,
The haunted, the night-watchers
Who can't wait any longer for morning, where are they going?

2.

Returning, revenant, I see Eighth Avenue is a poem,
Seventh and Broadway are epics, Fifth an extravaganza
From the winos and freaks at its feet in Washington Square
(Past once-white buildings, long-ago sidewalk cafés
Behind grimy privet, Fourteenth Street's brash interruption)
To the crossover at Twenty-third.
                                    At Thirty-fourth
The mammoth parade of department stores begins,
And, on the pavement, a cacophony of hawkers
That stretches beyond the stone lions, the bravura
Of Forty-second, to a kind of apotheosis
At Fifty-ninth.
                                    O prevalence of pinnacles!
O persistence of uniformed doormen sounding, in the rain,
Your lordly whistles! On Madison and Third
I am assaulted by florists' windows
Bursting with tropical blooms, I'm magnetized
By the windows of jewelry shops, by vegetables

Displayed like jewels, I'm buffeted
By the turbulence of this stream
Of life, this lyric, this mystery,
This daily miracle-play.

3.

What impossible collaborations
Are being consummated in cloud-high offices!
How many sweaty love-acrobatics are being performed
Behind a thousand windows
In the tall imperturbable hotels!
                                And all day long
The restless crowds continue in the street,
Ebbing and flowing like the tidal rivers,
And I am carried, flotsam like the rest,
Riding the crest of the flood down to the sea.

4.

Certain images I take with me,
Rescuing them from the flood;
Cast ashore, like so many others,
In a landscape I never imagined
But have come to recognize
I need something to define my life.

Coming back to the narrow island
Between the two rivers, on my right
The sweet river of memory,
And on my left the sweet river
Of forgetfulness, I see what I have become,
A woman in a blue dress,
Carried along on my own tides.

5.

Wherever I go, the river accompanies me;
It flows through my earliest dreams, its satiny surface
Fretted with lyrical little waves, or garnished
In winter, with baroque islands of ice.
Alongside, on the windswept upper deck
Of a bus, I rode to womanhood.
Now, around countless corners, in drafty offices,
Gleaming lobbies, or decorous apartments
Suspended in midair like the fabulous hanging
Gardens, I breathe its breath, and feel
Its salty undertow, tugging me home.

Calling the Nine Proud Walkers

There is no longer anyone who listens.
The voices are too insistent, there are too many
Clamoring to be heard, too many shouting,
Crying out, howling, bawling, and bellowing,
Too many mutterers, mumblers, stammerers,
Ranters and declaimers, tub-thumpers, spouters,
Incoherent babblers, gibberers, jabberers—
The wires are buzzing like an angry hive,
The airwaves, overloaded, can't transmit any more.

Silent, solitary in the starless night
I am besieged by invisible regiments,
The clamorous armies of the have-nothings.
Where are the nine proud walkers
Who might have smoothed this discord into song?

The Creation

I see him up there; he has turned his back on the world;
Hunched over the drawing-board, he is making it new
All over again, every day
The same old story, starting over
From the beginning. First, of course, the garden.

His concentration is absolute, he is inventing
Broccolis, squashes, tomatoes, pumpkins, and peas,
Green Goliaths, Early Beauties, Sweet Mamas, Jade Crosses,
And the rain that will water them, and the sun
That will shine down on them.

When he looks up, I know we see the same bird
Silhouetted against a backdrop of bristling mountains—
Not gentle little hills like sheep in a meadow—
A single bird, flashing at the tip of a twig
Like a tiny flame, like a flickering tongue of fire,

And he is inventing fire: under his pencil
Now lightning stabs the horizon, and thunder rumbles
Out of the distant mountains over the plain
Where the heavy clouds of his imagination
Perpetually ripen, pregnant with mystery.

Notes

Page 3: "a kitchen knife . . ." and "plunged his hands . . ." are translations of what de Maupassant wrote about Courbet and Monet, quoted in *The Lost World of the Impressionists,* by Alice Bellony-Rewald. Mexico "seems a motif . . ." is from *Frida: A Biography of Frida Kahlo,* by Hayden Herrera.

Page 4: "the drive to live . . ." and "a dry crust . . ." are from *The Devil Drives,* by Fawn M. Brodie.

Page 5: The wire-walker quoted is Karl Wallenda, who was killed in a fall from the high wire in 1978.

Page 8: Mr. and Mrs. Payne and the elephants were in a *New York Times* article, 11 February 1986. Dr. Gibo was in *Travel/Vistas,* 10 November 1985.

Page 10: "lunatic laundresses" from *The Female Malady,* by Elaine Showalter.

Page 21: "resembling the vibrations . . ." is from a newspaper article on earthquakes.

About the Author

Constance Urdang was born in New York City. She has a BA from Smith College and an MFA from the University of Iowa. She is the author of eight volumes of poetry and fiction, including *The Lone Woman and Others* and *Only the World,* both published in the Pitt Poetry Series. Among her awards is a National Endowment for the Arts Poetry Fellowship and the Delmore Schwartz Memorial Poetry Award. She divides her year between St. Louis, Missouri, and San Miguel de Allende, Mexico.

PITT POETRY SERIES

Ed Ochester, General Editor